What's in the House?
Pamela Wakefield

January 2020
March 2021

Printed in the United States of America.

That He might present it to himself a glorious church, not having spot, or wrinkle, or any such thing; but that it should be holy and without blemish.

Ephesians 5:27

For the Lord himself will come down

from heaven, with a loud command,

with the voice of the archangel and with

the trumpet call of God, and the dead in

Christ will rise first. After that, we who

are still alive and are left will be caught

up together with them in the clouds to

meet the Lord in the air. And so we will

be with the Lord forever.

1 Thessalonians 4:16-17

Table of Contents
◆ ◆ ◆ ◆ ◆ ◆ ◆

Author's Preface

♦ ♦ ♦ ♦ ♦ ♦

There is an urgent cry to the body of Christ! We must be ready for Jesus return and be the church God has called us to be. *Therefore, be ye also ready, for the Son of Man is coming at an hour you do not expect* (Matthew 24:44*).*

As born-again believers, one of our main responsibilities is to witness and lead others to Jesus Christ. The Bible says in Matthew 28: 19-20, "Therefore go and make disciples of all nations, baptizing them in the name of the Father and of the Son and of the Holy Spirit, and teaching them to obey everything I have commanded you. And surely, I am with you always, to the very end of the age." My heart's desire is that we make every opportunity to share salvation and the Good News of Jesus Christ with others. It is also our responsibility to live the life God has called us to live. If we want to go higher in God and want to see His Glory manifested in our lives and in the churches. We have to allow God to examine the condition of our hearts.

I believe in order for the church to grow spiritually and where God wants us to be, we have to take inventory of what's in our hearts. The world is watching us, but most of all God is watching. We are to be a light in a dark world.

Our desire as believers is to see God's Kingdom manifested on earth, as it's already done in Heaven. This book is not intended for us to look at others, and judge their walk, or bring condemnation, but allow God to examine the condition of our hearts so we can walk in God's truth.

In order for us to be followers of Jesus Christ. We have to take on His nature by walking in obedience, holiness and His righteousness. For we are made partakers of Christ, if we hold the beginning of our confidence steadfast unto the end (Hebrews 3:14).

God wants us to be true disciples for Him. Therefore, transformation must take place within us. We must discipline (crucify) our minds and bodies to be led by the Spirit and not our sinful nature (the flesh). We must pick up our cross and follow Him. "Jesus told his disciples, "'If anyone would come after me, let him deny himself and take up his cross daily and follow me" (Matthew 16:24).

God is looking for true worshipers who will worship Him in Spirit and in truth. (John 4:24). We can't just talk the talk. God is calling us to walk the walk. The people of God will have to rise to the occasion by standing for holiness and truth. He is looking for us to be an example of Him in the earth.

God desires that no one should perish but have eternal life with Him. Therefore, our relationship with God is not based on our works, tradition, titles, positions, offices, or how long we've been attending church. Our relationship with God should be a heartfelt, sincere desire to be more like Christ.

We live in a world where people are hurting and broken. They are looking for truth, love, and acceptance. They need people who can be real, nonjudgmental, loving, compassionate, genuine, and kind. They realize the world can't satisfy their pain, so they are turning to Jesus.

In the midst of their despair they are looking for a church (a people) where love is displayed. Christians live what they preach, healing takes place, captives are set free, blinded eyes are made to see, the lame walk, and hope is offered to the hopeless. Therefore, we must be ready and in position to receive people with open arms and a loving heart. A heart that pleases God.

It's so important that we take the time to allow God to examine the condition of our hearts so that we have a heart to please God and we won't become a stumbling block to those who are looking for love and acceptance through Jesus Christ.

We can ask ourselves some serious questions: When people look at me will they see an image of Jesus Christ? Are my behaviors and actions reflecting the love of Jesus Christ? Is the Fruit of the Spirit operating in my life? Is Jesus pleased with me? Is my heart acceptable unto Him? If Jesus came back today, would I be ready?

Introduction

♦ ♦ ♦ ♦ ♦

On March 9, 2003, I began writing this book and it was an ongoing process. I can remember when God started speaking to me about writing this book. It started with me reading and meditating on His Word, that He began revealing *me to me*.

He revealed to me in 2003, that I lacked patience, had selfish ambitions and had issues with anger. God guided me to Galatians 5:19-21, which says, "The acts of the sinful nature are obvious: sexual immorality, impurity and debauchery; idolatry and witchcraft; hatred, jealousy, fits of rage, selfish ambition, dissensions (discord, malice, conflict) factions (cliques, self-seeking, contentious) and envy; drunkenness, orgies, and the like. I warn you, as I did before, that those who live like this will not inherit the Kingdom of God."

God began showing me how I attended Bible study on Wednesdays, church on Sundays, ushered, and served on church committees, and that even though I was doing good things in the church, I had some inner work that needed to be done.

I thought just because I was serving, speaking in tongues, falling out in the spirit and trying to please God, I was okay. Wrong! I wasn't okay. The truth of the matter is that God revealed that I had issues that was hold me back from inheriting His promises, if I continued living like that. Sometimes, there are "things" hidden within us that we are unaware of and are driving our behaviors and displeases God. And these "things" will continue to resurface in our lives, and have us going around the circles, leaving us unfruitful and unproductive, if we don't change.

Those hidden things can be: hurt from the past, disappointments, despair, sorrow, unforgiveness, rebellion, control, hatred, judging others, rejection, abandonment, hatred, anger, bitterness, resentment, jealousy, envy, greed, anxiety, fear, worry, fear of what others will think, distrust, doubt, pride, ego, fault-finding, self-righteous, self-will, indecisiveness, self-pity, confusion, double mindedness, lust, perversion, frustration, impatience, shame, condemnation, backbiting, gossiping, and the like. It's imperative that we ask Holy Spirt to reveal what's hidden in our hearts and the things that displeases God, which doesn't give Him glory and is hindering our love walk.

The enemy doesn't mind keeping us blinded from the truth. He will continue to keep us busy, even in our churches and ministries, so we won't discover what's hidden within us. We must be mindful not to be so busy doing stuff that we fail to spend time with the Father so He can reveal what maybe hidden in our hearts.

When we slow down, quiet ourselves and spend time with God and meditate on His Word. He will reveal what's in our hearts. Sometimes we can be so busy with the cares of the world, and serving and ministering to others that we fail to take time to slow down and quiet ourselves and let God speak to us about us.

God cares and desires that we have fruitful and productive lives. He will reveal what's hidden so we can address the matter and allow Holy Spirit to do the work. The enemy wants us to stay blinded, bounded and ignorant of his devices, so that he can continue to use those things against us and keep us unfruitful. He doesn't want us to be free, but whom the Son sets free is free indeed (John 8:36).

I will not forget what God did for me on that day. God talked to me about my sinful nature so that I would acknowledge it, repent, and invite the Holy Spirit to help me to change. When I started writing this book, I can't tell you how many times I procrastinated. But on May 20, 2004, God became serious with me. He told me that the blood would be on my hands if I didn't tell His people what He told me to tell them. So, I began writing again. It reminded me of the Scripture in Ezekiel 3:18-19 in which God told the prophet Ezekiel:

> When I say unto the wicked, Thou shalt surely die; and thou givest him not warning, nor speakest to warn the wicked from his wicked way, to save his life; the same wicked man shall die in his iniquity; but his blood will I require at thine hand. Yet if thou warn the wicked, and he turn not from his wickedness, nor from his wicked way, he shall die in his iniquity; but thou hast delivered thy soul.

Therefore, on August 25, 2005, after many tears and asking God to forgive me for procrastinating, I made a commitment to continue writing. And now I see the vision more clearly. God's love and heartbeat for mankind is that no man shall be separated from Him, but have everlasting fellowship with Him forever.

I invite you to open your hearts and minds and allow God to help you meditate upon the condition of your heart. You may be thinking that everything is okay, but it's beneficial to allow God to reveal what maybe hidden in your heart. God desires that we have a change of heart so that we can inherit His promises now and eternally.

The time is now for us to step up and be the church, the people God has called us to be. A house that is free from clutter, one that is holy and obedient to the Holy Spirit. God wants us to grow in Him so His will can be manifested on earth as it is already in heaven. We can't go to the next level or dimension in God if we continue to allow our flesh to lead and govern our lives.

The Spirit of God is seeking a clean house to dwell in, and not a house full of rage, anger, slander, unforgiveness, backbiting, gossip, malice, strife, haughtiness, hatred, jealousy, lying, greed, pride, envy, selfish ambitions, self-righteous, disobedient, rebellion, uncleanness, homosexuality, fornication, adultery, lust, drunkenness, perversion, sexual immoralities, and so forth. God warns us in Galatians 5:19-21: "those who live like this will not inherit the kingdom of God."

God cannot pour out His blessings upon us if we continue to walk in disobedience. He wants us to be a blessed generation. Deuteronomy 11:26-28 states, "See, I am setting before you today a blessing and a curse—the blessing if you obey the commands of the LORD your God that I am giving you today; the curse if you disobey the commands of the LORD your God and turn from the way that I command you today by following other gods, which you have not known."

God gives us free will to make choices. The Bible says, "Everything is permissible for me—but not everything is beneficial" (1 Corinthians 6:12). God wants us to choose those things that will bring us good and not harm. He won't force us to do anything. He will leave the decisions up to us.

I wrote this book to speak truth—God's truth! I know everyone won't like this message, but this book wasn't written to please the masses. It was written to bring about change in the lives of those who have a spiritual ear to hear what God is saying to the church. God is love and His desire is that His glory is manifested in the Earth and that we return back to Him with a clean heart.

God cannot use us as His vessels if we continue to turn a deaf ear to Him and His commands. "If a man therefore purge himself from these, he shall be a vessel unto honour, sanctified, and meet for the master's use, and prepared unto every good work" (2 Timothy 2:21) In order to live life victoriously in Christ Jesus, we must be led by the Holy Spirit and not by our sinful nature. Our issues, habits, vices, emotions, and so forth will keep us sinning if we don't check ourselves.

God is willing to help us, but are we willing to give up those things and people that so easily lead us astray? God will allow reminders and behaviors to continue to keep showing up in our lives, about us, - to let us know that there is something that needs to be changed. The same old issue(s) will keep resurfacing in our lives until we decide to address them and have a change of heart. He will give us time to repent and turn away from those things that will so easily lead us astray.

God desires the absolute best for our lives. He is a loving, merciful, and patient God who gives us chances after chances to get things right. He gives us brand new mercies every day. God loves us more than we love ourselves. Think about it. God loves us so very much that He gives us opportunities to take heed, before it's too late. Some of us have been attending church Sunday after Sunday and carrying the same old stuff for years. He wants us to be free. He desires that we benefit from His promises, but in order for us to inherit His promises, we must be in right relationship with Him.

I pray that you allow God to take inventory of your heart and take hold to whatever God has called you to do. Obey Him. Repent of your sins and make a decision to allow the Holy Spirit to reveal what's in your heart and any sinful areas. Don't allow sin, pride, or disobedience separate you from God or His promises. "Behold, I stand at the door, and knock: if any man hear my voice, and open the door, I will come in to him, and will sup with him, and he with me" (Revelation3:20).

My brothers and sisters, my prayer is that you commit to God totally – mind, body, and spirit – and obey God's Word. "Not that I have already obtained all this, or have already arrived at my goal, but I press on to take hold of that for which Christ Jesus took hold of me. Brothers [and sisters], I do not consider myself yet to have taken hold of it. But one thing I do: Forgetting what is behind and straining toward what is ahead, I press on toward the goal to win the prize for which God has called me heavenward in Christ Jesus" (Philippians 3:12-14).

Chapter 1

It Starts with Salvation

♦ ♦ ♦ ♦ ♦ ♦ ♦

Therefore, my dear friends, as you have always obeyed—not only in my presence, but now much more in my absence—continue to work out your salvation with fear and trembling, for it is God who works in you to will and to act according to his good purpose.
Philippians 2:12-13)

I remember accepting Jesus Christ as my Lord and Savior when I was a teenager. But when I was in my thirties, I rededicated my life back to Jesus Christ and became a born-again believer. I was so excited! I wanted to tell everybody about my newfound love and what I'd experienced. I realized that my confession to accept Jesus Christ as my Savior was the beginning of my Christian walk.

Our road to salvation doesn't just equate to one being baptized. It continues after we made our confession for salvation so that a transformation can take place in our hearts and then we will see an outward change. It starts in the heart. The Bible states in Romans 10:9-10, "That if thou shalt confess with thy mouth the Lord Jesus, and shalt believe in thine heart that God hath raised him from the dead, thou shalt be saved. For with the heart man believeth unto righteousness, and with the mouth confession is made unto salvation."

Salvation doesn't stop with a confession but continues by one being born again of the Spirit so that transformation can take place in our lives. Jesus told Nicodemus in John 3:3, "I tell you the truth, no one can see the Kingdom of God unless he is born again." When we begin the process of being born again, we begin taking on a new nature, the nature of Jesus Christ. We become followers of Jesus Christ. We become Christ like. We start dying to our flesh and start living by the Spirit. "I will give them an undivided heart and put a new spirit in them; I will remove from them their heart of stone and give them a heart of flesh. Then they will follow my decrees and be careful to keep my laws. They will be my people, and I will be their God" (Ezekiel 11:19-20).

If we have a desire in our hearts for change, our behaviors will change. We will take on a new walk and new talk. We will no longer desire to live the life of the sinful/carnal man but live the life Christ desires for us. His desire will become our desire. His will, will become our will. His pleasures will become our pleasures. His way of living will become our way of living.

Quite often, we confess salvation and say we love the Lord, but our actions display the opposite of what He desires. When

God looks at His creation, He is not always pleased with what He sees. Jesus said, "If you love me, keep my commandments (John 14:15).

Salvation is a gift from God, and it should not be taken lightly. Salvation is not a gift that you open, place on a shelf, and do nothing with it. Our salvation walk should cultivate us into spiritual maturity and transformation as we are obedient to the Father. Our perseverance toward spiritual maturity is ongoing. It's a new way of living. It's a new beginning for the rest of our lives. Philippians 2:12 tells us to "continue to work out your soul's salvation with fear and trembling." When we allow God to expose what is hidden in our hearts, transformation and sanctification can take place. John 8:32 states, "Then you will know the truth, and the truth will set you free."

We must be aware of the war waging within us, our sinful nature battling our spirit. The sinful man versus the spiritual man. Galatians 5:17 states, "For the flesh desires what is contrary to the Spirit, and the Spirit is contrary to the flesh. They are in conflict with each other, so that you are not to do whatever you want." The good news is that when we become born again, we have access to the Holy Spirit to lead and guide us into truth and assist us in combating evil and empowering us to take authority and dominion over our sinful nature and embracing God's truth.

Therefore, when our sinful nature tells us something contrary to the Word of God, we can take authority over our thoughts by speaking God's truth over the matter and make a decision to follow truth. In the Bible, each time Satan tempted Jesus, He was able to combat the negative forces of evil by speaking a biblical truth to counteract the negative. The sinful nature is not going down without a fight. It will struggle to stand its ground.

Romans 7:18-25 states:

I know that nothing good lives in me, that is, in my sinful nature. For I have the desire to do what is good, but I cannot carry it out. For what I do is not the good I want to do; no, the evil I do not want to do—this I keep on doing. Now if I do what I do not want to do, it is no longer I who do it, but it is sin living in me that does it. So I find this law at work: When I want to do good, evil is right there with me. For in my inner being I delight in God's law; but I see another law at work in the members of my body, waging war against the law of my mind and making me a prisoner of the law of sin at work within my members. What a wretched man I am! Who will rescue me from this body of death? Thanks be to God through Jesus Christ our Lord! So then, I myself in my mind am a slave to God's law, but in the sinful nature a slave to the law of sin.

Romans 8:5-8 also tells us, "Those who live according to the sinful nature have their minds set on what that nature desires, but those who live in accordance with the Spirit have their minds set on what the Spirit desires. The mind governed by the flesh of sinful man is death, but the mind controlled by the Spirit is life and peace. The sinful mind is hostile to God; it does not submit to God's law, nor can it do so. Those controlled by the sinful nature cannot please God."

It's important to read the Bible to get understanding. If you don't read the Bible, you can't reap the benefits of its wisdom and truth. Hosea 4:6 states, "My people are destroyed for lack of knowledge." The Bible is our guide for Christian living. "For the word of God is living and active. Sharper than any double-edged sword, it penetrates even to dividing soul and spirit, joints and marrow; it judges the thoughts and attitudes of the heart" (Hebrews 4:12).

It is time out for those feel-good sermons – the ones that make you feel good for the moment and send you right back home with the same old issues. It's time for yokes to be broken, strongholds to be demolished, and deliverance to take place. It's time for kingdom builders to step up and live the life God has called us to live. Pleasing the masses won't set anyone free; only the truth will set us free. God desires that His children live victoriously on earth, as well as live eternally with Him in heaven. But it's up to us to do our part. If the Son sets you free, you will be free indeed (John 8:36).

It doesn't matter if you have been called to be an apostle, prophet, evangelist, pastor, teacher, bishop, elder, minister, deacon, deaconess, trustee, usher, psalmist, or layperson. No one is exempt. If we say we are His and He is ours, we must obey Him. We can offer up to God all of our sacrifices and praises, but if we don't obey Him, we won't eat from the good of the land. The Scriptures tells us, "To obey is better than sacrifice" (1 Samuel 15:22). Each of us will be responsible for our own walk with Christ.

We are held accountable to God for what we do and what we do not do. Jesus says in Matthew 7:21-23, "Not everyone that saith unto me, Lord, Lord, shall enter into the kingdom of heaven; but he that doeth the will of my Father which is in heaven. Many will say to me in that day, Lord, Lord, have we not prophesied in thy name? and in thy name have cast out devils? and in thy name done many wonderful works? And then will I profess unto them, I never knew you: depart from me, ye that work iniquity."

Jesus has prophesied that many will come expecting their names to be written in the Lamb's book of life because they did good things, but their hearts were far from Him. God has given us free will to choose good or evil. The Bible clearly explains the benefits of living life by the Spirit, as well as the consequences of sin. God had a purpose and plan for the Israelites. He wanted to take them into the Promised Land, but because of their disobedience, many of them could not enter in and inherit all that God had promised them. God allowed many of them to die in the wilderness with their old ways of thinking and their sinful behaviors. We don't want to be like that generation. We want to inherit His promises, because His promises are yea and amen.

God will not let us inherit His promises if our houses are defiled. He desires that we inherit His promises, but because of our rebellious nature, He can't take us where He desires, until we turn around (repent) and change our ways. Second Chronicles 7:14 states, "If my people, who are called by my name, will humble themselves and pray and seek my face and turn from their wicked ways, then will I hear from heaven and will forgive their sin and will heal their land."

The sinful nature is outright defiant and rebellious toward God. It acts in disobedience. When we sin, we disobey God's instructions, laws, commands, and directives. Any time we disobey the voice of the Lord, we are sinning and not walking in agreement with Him. Sin doesn't just go away by wishing it away. We must repent. Sin separates us from God but thank God for His love, grace and mercy which allow us to repent and start over again.

For change to take place in our lives, we must allow the Holy Spirit to come into our lives and help change wrong thinking and behaviors. "Therefore, if any man be in Christ, he is a new creature: old things are passed away; behold, all things are become new (2 Corinthians 5:17). As we allow the Holy Spirit to guide and teach us God's ways, we will no longer immediately act on sinful desires but will lean more toward living according to God's principles.

Each of us must honestly examine our life and relationship with God. Therefore, consider these questions: If Jesus came back today, would you be ready? Or would He find you continuing living in sin and in disobedience?

Chapter 2

The House That Jacob Built

♦ ♦ ♦ ♦ ♦ ♦ ♦

"As for me and my household we are going to serve the Lord."
Joshua 24:15

In the book of Genesis, we find the life of Jacob and Esau, who were twin sons born to Isaac and Rebekah. The Bible states that Esau was born first, and Jacob was born second, and that Isaac loved Esau and Rebekah loved Jacob.

One day, Esau came in from hunting and was hungry. He felt if he didn't eat, he would die soon. His brother, Jacob, seized the moment and deceived Esau into selling him his birthright for something to eat. Esau gave up his birthright and inheritance for a temporary bout of hunger.

As their father, Isaac, grew older, and was blind and near death, he requested that his eldest son, Esau, bring him his favorite meal before he died so he could bless him.

Rebekah heard her husband's request and decided to take matters into her own hands. She convinced Jacob to disguise himself to look like Esau so he could receive his father's blessing, instead of Esau. Therefore, Rebekah cooked her husband's favorite meal and Jacob disguised himself and presented the meal to his father. And then Isaac asked Jacob, "Art thou my son Esau? And he said I am." Therefore, Isaac laid hands on his son Jacob, thinking he was Esau, and blessed Jacob and his seed instead.

After Esau realized that Jacob had deceived him once again, he wanted to kill Jacob. Rebekah warned Jacob to run and stay with her brother, Laban, until Esau was no longer angry at Jacob. Jacob fled and was welcomed into his uncle Laban's home. Laban had two daughters, Leah and Rachel. When Jacob saw Rachel, he desired to marry her. Laban agreed with the condition that Jacob would work for him for seven years for Rachel.

However, after the morning of the marriage, Jacob learned that Laban had deceived him into marrying his eldest daughter, Leah, instead of Rachel. Jacob was furious and asked Laban, "Why have you deceived me?" Laban explained that it was customary for the eldest daughter to wed first and that he would allow Jacob to marry Rachel if he would agree to complete his first week of marriage to Leah and work for him for another seven years for Rachel. This made Jacob a servant to Laban for many years. You might be thinking, good for Jacob; he got what he deserved. After all, look at how he deceived his brother, Esau, and his father, Isaac. Many of us would say Jacob reaped what he sown.

After Jacob's many years of servitude to Laban were over, the voice of the Lord told Jacob to return to his homeland and God would be with him. The Bible tells us that on his journey back home, Jacob sent his two wives, servants, children, and all that he had before him, and he spent the night alone on a riverside he named Peniel. The Bible says Jacob wrestled with the angel of God all night. "Then the man (angel) said, 'Let me go, for it is daybreak.' But Jacob replied, 'I will not let you go unless you bless me.' Jacob named the place Peniel, meaning, 'For I have seen God face to face, and yet my life has been delivered" (Genesis 32:22-32).

I believe before Jacob could return home he had to face his past. Jacob realized he needed God's help and intervention to face a brother he had deceived. The good news is that Jacob came to his senses. He didn't point any fingers or blame anyone else for his shortcomings. He came to the end of himself.

Only the touch of the Father and a willing heart can make a person abandon his or her sinful ways. Jacob's sinful house was built on: greed, lies, trickery, schemes and deception, but it didn't stay that way. He understood he needed to be changed. He needed deliverance. Truth and desperation drove Jacob to the place of seeking God with his whole heart. He humbled himself to the power of the almighty God.

After Jacob's encounter with the angel of God, he returned to his homeland and was reconciled with his brother. The Bible tells us that when Esau saw Jacob coming towards him, he ran to him, embraced and kissed him, and they wept. How awesome is our God!

So many times, we often reap seeds that were sown in our lives through our own hands, or those of our ancestors. Nevertheless, these same seeds keep springing up in our lives as sin. The truth of the matter is that whatever type of seeds you have sown, or were sown by your ancestors, they could possibly impact your life and/or the lives of your children or your children's children, until somebody breaks the curse and change their course of direction. Thou shalt not bow down thyself unto them, nor serve them: for I the Lord thy God am a jealous God, visiting the iniquity of the fathers upon the children unto the third and fourth generation of them that hate me. And showing mercy unto thousands of them that love me and keep my commandments. (Hebrews 5:9-10).

The act of what we are sow will produce fruit, and if we are not producing good fruit, it is time to change the kinds of seeds (behaviors) we are sowing in order to reap a different type of harvest. The Bible tells us, "The fruit of the Spirit is love, joy, peace, patience, kindness, goodness, faith, gentleness and self-control; against such there is no law. And they that are Christ's have crucified the flesh with the affections and lusts. If we live in the Spirit, let us also walk in the Spirit" (Galatians 5:22-25).

Our sinful behaviors such as: greed, pride, envy, jealousy, sexual immoralities, fornication, adultery, lust, perversion, lying, gossiping, selfishness, bitterness, hatred, anger, resentment, rebellion, disobedience, strife, stealing, confusion, self-righteousness, lack of self-control, manipulation, haughtiness, arrogance, impatient, selfishness, and the like will continue showing up in our lives and working against us, until we decide to change. He beckons, "Here I am! I stand at the door and knock. If anyone hears my voice and opens the door, I will come in and eat with him and he with me. To him who overcomes, I will give the right to sit with me on my throne, just as I overcame and sat down with my Father on his throne" (Revelation 3:20-21).

The choice to serve the Lord is an individual decision. Jacob made a decision to change when he cried out to God! His actions were affirmed! "As for me and my household we are going to serve the Lord" (Joshua 24:15). Each of us must choose whom we will serve. When we are ready for change and are tired of having the same outcomes and living a life outside of the will of God. We will make up our minds and decide to stop everything to have an encounter with God so that our lives will change for the better. God will work on our behalf if we are truly ready to change and move forward with Him.

When we come clean with God and be honest, God can begin the work within us. God knows the hearts of His children. And in the life of Jacob, Jacob had an encounter with God because he desired to be changed. Hence, God gave Jacob a new beginning and a new name. God changed Jacob's name from deceiver to Israel, which meant, "he struggled with God and men and overcame" (Genesis 32:28). And in the same way, God can give us a new beginning too, if we truly desire it.

Chapter 3

Taming the Tongue

♦ ♦ ♦ ♦ ♦ ♦ ♦

Do not let any unwholesome talk come out of your mouths, but only what is helpful for building others up according to their needs, that it may benefit those who listen.
Ephesians 4:29

As Christians, we must be careful what comes out of our mouths. We can do more harm than good with our untamed tongues and meaningless conversations. The Bible says, "The tongue is also a fire, a world of evil among the parts of the body. It corrupts the whole person, sets the whole course of his life on fire, and is itself set on fire by hell. All kinds of animals, birds and reptiles and creatures of the sea are being tamed and have been tamed by man, but no man can tame the tongue. It is a restless evil, full of deadly poison" (James 3:6-8).

God is not pleased when we use profanity, gossip, lie, slander, and speak curses and negativity over people lives. And He is also not pleased with how we talk to one another, the tone we use, and the words we say. God wants us to be mindful of our conversations. We are to be a light in a dark world and our behaviors should be set apart from the world. But many times, our conversations are no different than the world's conversations. God

27

wants our conversations to be inspirational, encouraging, edifying, uplifting and purposeful. "With the tongue we praise our Lord and Father, and with it we curse men, who have been made in God's likeness. Out of the same mouth come praising and cursing. My brothers, this should not be" (James 3:9-10).

When we allow our sinful nature to lead our conversations, we don't have victory but defeat. Trying to tame the tongue is not easy. It will require discipline and the Holy Spirit assisting us by leading and guiding our conversations. Sometimes our negative conversations are derived from habit, hurt, pain, frustration, stress, emotions, anger, hatred, bitterness, resentment, jealousy or envy. "For out of the abundance of the mouth, the heart speaketh" (Luke 6:45).

If we are not careful, we can tear others down with our tongues, instead of edifying, encouraging and lifting them up. Have you ever taken the time to reflect on how many people you may have hurt with your unkind or harsh words or tone. Any time our speech doesn't line up with the Word of God and the leading of Holy Spirit, we don't glorify God and could be hurting others.

I have also noticed that sometimes we use inappropriate language and profanity as if it means nothing to God. This type of behavior grieves the Holy Spirit. The Bible says, "Do not let any unwholesome talk come out of your mouths, but only what is helpful for building others up according to their needs, that it may benefit those who listen" (Ephesians 4:29). Using profanity does not give God glory, nor is it wholesome or edifying. Proverbs 4:24 states, "Put away perversity from your mouth; keep corrupt talk far from your lips."

We also have problems with gossiping. Some believers seem to be confused in this area because they think it's okay to gossip, as long as they believe the information is to be true. Wrong! Anytime you are unnecessarily talking about someone's intimate and personal affairs, you are gossiping. "The Bible says, "A perverse man stirs up dissension, and gossiper separates close friends" (Proverbs 16:28). We have to be mindful that our conversations, inside and outside of the church, should reflect the nature and heartbeat of God.

I can remember talking to an individual and asking him why he didn't go to church. He replied that one of the reasons was because "church people" tend to gossip too much. I understood what he meant, but it was disheartening to hear. There are people who really need and have a desire to come to our churches but decide against it because of their negative experiences in the church. We have to be careful not to be a stumbling block or hindrance to others.

Slander is another issue we must address. We can confuse gossip and slander. Although they are very much alike, gossip is talking about another person's personal or intimate affairs, while slander is making false, and often injurious, statements that can negatively impact a person's reputation or character. We don't want to take pleasure in listening to slanderous reports or willingly join or helping to spread the rumor. The next time someone comes to you with a slanderous report, change the course of the discussion, and say to the person bringing the slanderous report: "Instead of talking about this, let's pray about it." You will find out where that person's heart is by watching how they respond to the statement. Each time we engage in spreading a false report, God will hold us just as accountable as the one who started the rumor. One of God's commandments in Exodus 23:1 says, "Do not spread false reports. Do not help a wicked man [person] by being a malicious witness."

If we spend less time talking about someone else and more time praying, studying our Bibles, working on our salvation, and examining our hearts, we will have less confusion inside and outside of our churches. It's time to stop peeping in someone else's door and start sweeping around our own doors.

Matthew 7:1-5 tells us:

Do not judge, or you too will be judged. For in the same way you judge others, you will be judged, and with the measure you use, it will be measured to you. Why do you look at the speck of sawdust in your brother's eye and pay no attention to the plank in your own eye? How can you say to your brother, let me take the speck out of your eye, when all the time there is a plank in your own eye? You hypocrite, first take the plank out of your own eye, and then you will see clearly to remove the speck from your brother's eye.

God also revealed that some of us talk too much. Our tongues go on and on just like the Duracell bunny: it just keeps "going and going." How can we hear what the Holy Spirit is saying if we are constantly talking? "My dear brothers, take note of this: Everyone should be quick to listen, slow to speak and slow to become angry" (James 1:19). God wants us to learn to listen more. Jesus gave us a perfect example of how to respond in a matter. In, John 8:3-7, when the Pharisees brought a woman to Jesus who was caught in adultery, the old law stated that any woman caught in adultery would be stoned to death. The people asked Jesus, "Teacher, this woman was caught in the act of adultery. In the Law, Moses commanded us to stone such women. Now what do you say?" Jesus did not respond quickly.

The Bible tells us that Jesus started writing on the ground with His finger, and then He responded and said, "If any one of you is without sin, let him be the first to throw a stone at her." The Bible further tells us that they all left, implying that not one of

31

them was without sin. Jesus didn't jump up as soon as He was questioned and reacted in a way that was abrupt, impulsive, or out of control. He responded in patience and love and offered the best answer. God wants us to be effective. If we can learn to slow down and listen to what the Spirit is telling us to say, we could be better witnesses for Jesus. My dear brothers and sisters, take note of this: Everyone should be quick to listen, slow to speak, and slow to become angry (James 1:19).

A lying tongue is another issue we must address. Do you know God despises lies? He hates them. "The Lord detests lying lips, but He delights in men who are truthful" (Proverbs 12:22).

Backbiting and quarreling are also harmful. Sometimes, we can get so caught up in disagreements and arguing that we end up saying words that are hurtful and that we eventually regret. "If you keep on biting and devouring each other, watch out or you will be destroyed by each other" (Galatians 5:15).

The world would be so much better if we would begin to work on taming our tongues and speak words of love, instead of words that lead to anger and hate. It is also important that we be aware of the tone we use.

Sometimes we can turn people off and hurt their feelings because we are harsh rather than gentle. "A soft and gentle and thoughtful answer turns away wrath, but harsh and painful and careless words stir up anger" (Proverbs 15:1). "For the wrath of man worketh not the righteousness of God" (James 1:20). We have to learn to talk in a tamer tone and remember to speak to each other in love, respect and in a gentler and kinder voice.

Chapter 4

Controlling Your Emotions

♦ ♦ ♦ ♦ ♦ ♦ ♦

Get rid of all bitterness, rage, and anger, brawling and slander, along
with every form of malice. Be kind and compassionate to one another,
forgiving each other, just as in Christ God forgave you.
Ephesians 4:31-32

Have you heard the saying, "The battlefield is in the
mind"? Well, it is. The mind is driven by our thoughts,
imaginations, and perceptions that lead our behaviors. The mind is
one of the devices the enemy uses against us. The mind will have
us thinking and responding in ways contrary to the Word of God.
The Apostle Paul tells us in Romans 12:2, "And be not conformed
to this world: but be ye transformed by the renewing of your mind,
that ye may prove what is that good, and acceptable, and perfect,
will of God."

We can't be the people God wants us to be if we continue
to have ill feelings toward one another. We must allow Holy Spirit
to teach us how to walk in love, joy, peace, patience, kindness,
goodness, faithfulness, gentleness and self-control. The enemy
loves to cause division and conflict in our lives, homes, families,
and in the church. The enemy does not like it when we have peace

and work on one accord. Satan will use anyone and anything to stir up dissension and discord. All it takes is one person to stir up confusion. It can be someone in your church or in your family.

On Sunday mornings, we sing songs about love, but often times we don't see love in operation for our fellow brother and sister in Christ. The Bible tells us in 1 John 4:20-21, "If anyone says, I love God, yet hates his brother, he is a liar. For anyone who does not love his brother, whom he has seen, cannot love God, whom he has not seen.

And he has given us this command: Whoever loves God must also love his brother." Ephesians 4:31-32 further explains that we must "Get rid of all bitterness, rage, and anger, brawling and slander, along with every form of malice. Be kind and compassionate to one another, forgiving each other, just as Christ forgave you."

Therefore, if we love God, we cannot hate our fellow brothers and sisters. First Peter 3:8-11 tells us, "Finally, all of you, live in harmony with one another; be sympathetic, love as brothers, be compassionate and humble. Do not repay evil with evil or insult with insult, but with blessing, because to this you were called so that you may inherit a blessing."

Sometimes we may have a hard time forgiving others, but if we want God to forgive us, we must forgive others. Matthew 6:15 strengthens this point by telling us, "But if you don't forgive men their sins, your Father will not forgive your sins." Quite often, many of us hold onto past hurt and anger about what someone has said or done to us, and we haven't forgiven them. We must release those feelings of unforgiveness so healing can take place and we can be free. Holding on to past hurt can cause us to become emotionally, physically, or spiritually ill. If we want to walk in freedom, we have to let go and allow God to heal the pain and help us to forgive those who have hurt us or done us wrong.

I had people in my life who lied on me and betrayed me. It was a hurtful experience, but I had to make a decision. Was I going to continue in unforgiveness, or was I going to allow God to help me to forgive? I knew I needed His help, because I couldn't do it on my own. The Father had to take me through the steps of forgiveness. I took my hurt and pain to Jesus and talked to Him about it. I talked less about the hurt and prayed more. The task wasn't easy, but it was possible because God was with me. I had to trust that God would take care of the matter, and He did. He healed my heart and comforted me. God allowed me to forgive others in spite of what they had said or done. I could not walk in freedom with old things from my past holding me down.

Anger and rage are emotions that are closely related. Rage could be fueled by unresolved anger about oneself or what someone else has done to you or your loved one. Anger is a natural emotion and response that we all can experience, but God warns us to settle the matter quickly and make amend so our anger won't grow into rage. Therefore, the Bible clearly tells us in Ephesians 4:26-27, "In your anger do not sin. Do not let the sun go down while you are still angry, and do not give the devil a foothold." James 1:20 states, "For man's anger does not bring about the righteous life that God desires."

Another issue we must address in the body of Christ is jealousy, envy, and greed. It's grievous when our brothers and sisters in Christ are jealous over each other's gifts, callings, anointings, or what others may have or be doing. I know it saddens the Father when we behave this way or are in competition with one another. We are supposed to be joyful, cheering each other on, and praying for each other, while we push God's mandate so that His Kingdom will be manifested in the earth. But many times, we see jealousy, envy, and greed at work.

We have to be careful that we don't become envious of what others have and what they are doing. We are to be thankful and grateful for what we have. There is nothing wrong with having nice things, because God wants us to be blessed. But when we desire material things for the wrong reasons, we must search our hearts and ask some hard questions. What are my motives for desiring these things? Do I want it for the right reasons, or do I want it because someone else has it?

We also want to make sure that we are not putting anything before God. We cannot worship or idolize our homes, automobiles, clothes, jobs, careers, spouses, family members, friends, pastor, or leaders and etc...

The Bible tells us in Exodus 20:3-6:

You shall have no other gods before me. You shall not make for yourself an idol in the form of anything in heaven above, or on the earth beneath or in the waters below. You shall not bow down to them or worship them; for I, the Lord your God, am a jealous God, punishing the children for the sin of the fathers to the third and fourth generation of those who hate me, but showing love to a thousand generations of those who love me and keep my commandments.

Any time we put an object or person before God, it is considered idolatry. It doesn't matter if it's your spouse, father, mother, children, sister, brother, boyfriend, girlfriend, employer, an individual, car, object, image, belief, house, job, or so on. Anything or anyone we adore, or worship excessively becomes a personal idol. It is a sin to place anyone or anything before God.

He must be first, and anything or anyone that we put before God will not last.

Another concern we must address is being anxious. An inpatient person is more prone to make hasty and impulsive decisions, but the Bible makes it clear in Philippians 4:6-7, "Do not be anxious about anything, but in everything, by prayer and petition, with thanksgiving, present your requests to God. And the peace of God, which transcends all understanding, will guard your hearts and your minds in Christ Jesus."

When we make hasty, impulsive, and emotional decisions instead of waiting on God, we are not giving the matter careful consideration and not waiting on God to respond. Being anxious and rushing into something can cause you to make decisions and choices you may regret later. When we don't wait on God, we end up with a mess. The Bible tells us in Proverbs 4:7, "Wisdom is the principal thing; therefore, get wisdom: and with all thy getting get understanding.

I've learned that it's better to wait on God and seek His face for wisdom regarding the situation. The Bible tells us in James 1:5, if you don't have wisdom ask God. "I any of you lacks wisdom, you should ask God, who gives generously to all without finding fault, and it will be given to you." God knows the plan for your life. His plan is the best plan. He wants our lives to be blessed. If God says, "wait," then wait. If He says, "no," it means no. If He says, "go," then go. Obey God!

Chapter 5

Fleeing Sexual Immoralities

♦ ♦ ♦ ♦ ♦ ♦ ♦

Flee from sexual immorality. All other sins a man commits are outside of his body, but he who sins sexually sins against his own body. Do you not know that your body is a temple of the Holy Spirit, who is in you, whom you have received from God? You are not your own; you were brought at a price. Therefore, honor God with your body.
1 Corinthians 6:18-20

Adultery, fornication, lust, homosexuality, pornography, and other sexual immoralities are sweeping the nation, and their influences are affecting Christians of all ages. God's design and purpose for sexual relations have been perverted. He created sexual intimacy and relationship between a husband and wife only.

Adultery is a sexual immorality we must discuss. I have heard Christians trying to justify that it's okay to have an adulterous relationship. But we must be clear, no matter how we may feel about it, God will not go against His Word.

But since there is so much immorality, each man should have his own wife, and each woman her own husband. The husband should fulfill his marital duty to his wife, and likewise the wife to her husband. The wife's body does not belong to her alone but also to her husband. In the same way, the husband's body does not belong to him alone but also his wife. (1 Corinthians 7:2-4)

"You shall not covet your neighbor's house. You shall not covet your neighbor's wife, or his male or female servant, his ox or donkey, or anything that belongs to your neighbor." (Exodus 20:17)

Fornication is another problem. Some may think they are justified in having premarital sex because God knows their needs and desires. Surely God knows our needs and desires, but we have to follow His principles and be in right standing with Him. First Peter 1:16 states, "Because it is written, be holy, for I am holy." The truth is, God knows about our sinful nature and will forgive our sins. But we can't continue to take advantage of God's forgiveness, love, grace, and mercy by continuing to fornicate intentionally and living a life of sin. God love us, but He will not continue to be mocked. If we are His children, we cannot expect God to continue to overlook our sinful ways, nor can we expect to escape the consequences of our behaviors if we continue disobeying Him and living a life that displeases and dishonors Him. "But fornication, and all uncleanness, or covetousness, let it not be once named among you, as becometh saints." (Ephesians 5: 3)

Each time we have a sexual relationship with someone other than our spouse, we are sinning. This also applies to those who are engaged. Engagement does not equate to marriage.

Engagement is the process and possibility leading to marriage. And, while you are in the process, you are not there yet. Therefore, an engaged person is a single person with the possibility of getting married. So until you say, "I do," you can't. You are still unmarried and bound to God's law of abstinence. I know it's not easy being single and remaining celibate. But we have to strive for holiness. As single Christians we are to be mindful when we are dating that we don't place ourselves in compromising and vulnerable situations to be tempted to sin.

To all my single brothers and sisters in Christ, God calls us to live a celibate and holy lifestyle. As singles, we cannot live together as husband and wife and not be married, or perform sexual acts, such as: phone sex, masturbating, using dildos/vibrators, performing oral sex or other types of sexual acts, and think it's okay in the eyes of God. These acts are sinful and fall outside of the will of God for singles. Many of us were blind, but we know the truth. God honors sex in marriage only. Marriage is honorable among all, and the bed undefiled; but whoremongers and adulterers God will judge (Hebrews 13:4).

We don't have to keep repeating the same mistakes we did in the past. Sex outside of marriage dishonors God and our bodies. "Flee fornication: Every sin that a man doeth is without the body; but he that committeth fornication sinneth against his own body"

43

(1 Corinthians 6:18). "For the wages of sin is death, but the gift of God is eternal life in Christ Jesus our Lord" (Romans 6:23).

I had a conversation with a young woman years ago about premarital sex. She said it was too late for her because she had already engaged in premarital sex. I reassured her that it is never too late to correct an error. She could start where she is and make a decision to repent and turn away from sin, and let Holy Spirit help her walk in holiness. "For all have sinned and fall short of the glory of God, and all are justified freely by his grace through the redemption that came by Christ Jesus" (Romans 3:23-24).

Sex is everywhere, and its influences are having negative effects on our children. And as adults, we have to set an example for our youth. I have witnessed and heard stories about children and teenagers engaging in all types of sexual activities at an early age. They are visiting pornography sites on the Internet, engaging in sex early, watching inappropriate shows, listening to inappropriate music, engaging in sexual conversations on their cell phones and other types of inappropriate sexual behaviors. This is immoral, and our heavenly Father is not pleased with these actions.

Another issue worth discussing is homosexuality, which has caused much confusion in our society. Most of us know about the accounts of Adam and Eve and the creation of man and woman. Therefore, we know God created man for woman, and woman for man. Please understand, I'm not bashing anybody, because I am empathetic toward all people. However, I must speak truth. I am an ambassador of Jesus Christ and I believe in Him and in His word. God does not condone or support a homosexual lifestyle. This doesn't mean that God doesn't love people who are practicing a homosexual lifestyle, because God loves all of us, but He hates the sin. It goes against what He created.

Romans 1:25-27states;

They exchanged the truth of God for a lie and worshipped and served created things rather than the Creator—who is forever praised. Amen. Because of this, God gave them over to shameful lusts. Even their women exchanged natural relations for unnatural ones. In the same way, the men also abandoned natural relations for unnatural ones. In the same way, the men also abandoned natural relations with women and were inflamed with lust for one another. Men committed indecent acts with other men and received in themselves the due penalty for their perversion.

There may be different reasons as to why someone may struggle in the area of homosexuality. I am not here to judge, but possibly shed light on the matter. Sometimes inappropriate doors are opened in a child's life which can cause confusion regarding a person's sexual identify. Could it be that a child was sexually abused or touched inappropriately? Could it be a generational curse? Could it be from hurt that someone experienced in a relationship, and now they've decided to choose a relationship with the same sex? Could it be a choice? Or could it be something else? I may have not listed all the possible reasons, because I don't know them all. But I do know that God is a healer and deliverer if we want to be delivered. God can turn our lives around. He can wipe our slates clean and give us a new beginning and let the past stay in the past. He can take us through the purification and purging process if we let Him. We don't have to do it alone.

We all need God's forgiveness, love, grace, and mercy to see us through the challenges and issues we all face, no matter what state we are in. God is a God of compassion and love. And as the body of Christ we must show love to everyone, no matter what lifestyle they choose or situation they are in. We are not to judge, but love one another! "A new commandment I give unto you, that ye love one another; as I have loved you, that ye also love one another" (John 13:34).

Chapter 6

Taking Inventory—What's in Your Heart?

♦ ♦ ♦ ♦ ♦ ♦ ♦

"Blessed are the pure in heart, for they will see God."
Matthew 5:8

The Bible gives us several accounts about our sinful nature. Galatians 5:17 states, "For the sinful nature desires what is contrary to the Spirit, and the Spirit what is contrary to the sinful nature. They are in conflict with each other, so that you are not to do whatever you want." Romans 7:17 states, "As it is, it is no longer I myself who do it, but it is sin living in me. Romans 7:21 says, "So I find this law at work: Although I want to do good, evil is right there with me." The Bible tells us in Galatians 5:24 that "those who belong to Christ Jesus have crucified the sinful nature (flesh) with its passions and desires."

We must address what's in our hearts that lead our sinful behaviors. For this chapter's purpose I will relate the sinful house to the heart. The sinful house is similar to our physical houses. Can you think back to a time when your home needed a good cleaning? You wanted to get rid of the clutter and mess and clean out those dirty areas. Well, it is the same with our hearts. God desires for us to clean out those things that so easily beset us.

The Bible says in Proverbs 4:23, "Above all else, guard your heart, for everything you do flows from it." What a revelation! So think about it, the things that we say and do are derived from our hearts. We could be dealing with issues of: pride, rejection, hurt, abandonment, bitterness, resentment, unforgiveness, anger, rage, envy, jealousy, arrogance, haughtiness, trust issues, judgmental, self-righteousness, rebellion, condemnation, control, perversion, manipulation, despair, hopelessness, fear, and etc., and not be aware of it. When we are faced with negative behaviors, we have to ask God to reveal what's in our hearts that's guiding our behaviors, actions, thoughts, and our speech that doesn't give Him glory.

In chapter 2, I referenced Jacob's house being built on deception and greed. Jacob took inventory of what was in his heart and cried out to God to be changed. One day each of us, if we are willing, will look in the mirror and see the reflection that stands before us. Many times, the reflection in the mirror is not always pretty, but thanks be to God, each of us can be transformed into a spiritual house that God can use. We may not know what all the issues are, but God will reveal it, if we seek Him and desire to know the truth. "If a man therefore purge himself from these, he shall be a vessel unto honour, sanctified, and meet for the master's use, and prepared unto every good work." (2 Timothy 2-21).

I know it is so much easier to walk in our familiar ways than it is to change, but what will we gain? "For what is a man profited, if he shall gain the whole world, and lose his own soul? Or what shall a man give in exchange for his soul?" (Matthew 16:26).

In 2003, I recall meeting a wonderful Christian woman from the Bahamas. She imparted some important words to me. She said, *"As Christians, our lifestyles should exemplify Christ. Believers as well as unbelievers should be able to look at us and without us opening our mouths, know that we are Christians. If we are followers of Christ, then we should resemble Him in our walk, talk, thoughts, and actions. It should be manifested in our everyday living."* Her words put everything into perspective for me; they were heart changing. Her words echoed, "Christians should be living a Christ-like life all the time." And if we fall short of doing so, we can quickly humble ourselves and repent.

I know change is not easy, but God understands and sees our efforts. If we take one step, He will help us take the next. God promised that He would never leave us nor forsake us (Deuteronomy 31:6). The Bible also tells us, "We can do all things through Christ, who gives us strength" (Philippians 4:13). Nothing is impossible for God. In order for us to move forward in God, we must be obedient and acknowledge those things that keep resurfacing in our lives as sin and allow God to speak to our hearts. Don't be like the foolish builder who heard the Word but did not build his house on a solid foundation (the Word of God). The Bible gives us an example of a wise and a foolish builder. In Matthew 7:24-27, Jesus says:

> Therefore, everyone who hears these words of mine and puts them into practice is like a wise man who built his house on the rock. The rain came down, the streams rose, and the winds blew and beat against that house; yet it did not fall, because it had its foundation on the rock. But everyone who hears these words of mine and does not put them into practice is like a foolish man who built his house on sand. The rain came down, the streams rose, and the winds blew and beat against that house, and it fell with a great crash.

You may have areas in your life that you know are sinful and other areas that you are unaware of. I encourage you to pray and ask God to reveal any sin or behavior that is not pleasing in His sight.

Chapter 7

Present Yourself as a Living Sacrifice

♦ ♦ ♦ ♦ ♦ ♦ ♦

Therefore, I urge you, brothers, in view of God's mercy, to offer your bodies as living sacrifices, holy and pleasing to God—this is your spiritual act of worship.
Romans 12:1

It's time to lay everything that causes us to sin on the altar: our vices, behaviors, habits, attitudes, and present ourselves as a living sacrifice. When we are powerless, God is powerful. "Therefore, since we are surrounded by such a great cloud of witnesses, let us throw off everything that hinders and the sin that so easily entangles, and let us run with perseverance that race marked out for us" (Hebrews 12:1).

One of my relatives and I have had many conversations regarding the flesh and its desire to do what it wants to do. She said to me, "You know, Pam, I get so sick and tired of my flesh telling me what to do, that I am going to start yelling at my flesh to 'shut up!' As funny as it was, and we laughed. I understood exactly what she meant.

Sometimes you can get so sick and tired of your flesh acting out the same old behaviors and producing the same old outcomes that you say, "Enough is enough!" You begin to speak with authority by taking dominion over your thoughts and commanding your mind and body to line up with the Word of God. That is why the Bible tells us to renew our mind. Romans 12:2 says, "Do not conform any longer to the pattern of this world but be transformed by the renewing of your mind. Then you will be able to test and approve what God's will is—His good, pleasing and perfect will."

Once a negative or sinful thought enters our mind, we have the power to act on it or let it pass. We can choose to allow that thought to lead us to do what is right in the eyes of the Lord, or we can reject God's truth. If we desire to do what is right in the eyes of the Lord, but our thought pattern is opposite of the Word of God, we have to put that thought under subjection and not act upon it. Instead, we must speak the Word of God over those thoughts. Second Corinthians 10:5, further explains that we are to "cast down imaginations, and every high thing that exalteth itself against the knowledge of God and bringing into captivity every thought to the obedience of Christ." Romans 8:6-8 tells us, "The mind of sinful man is death, but the mind controlled by the Spirit is life and peace. The sinful mind is hostile to God. It does not submit to God's law, nor can it do so. Those controlled by the sinful nature cannot please God."

The sinful mind is so used to leading and telling the flesh what to do that it battles with our spirit to stay in control. When the sinful mind tells you something contrary to the Word of God, we must combat it with the Word of God. Remember, we are not doing this alone or in our own power. The Bible tells us that we are empowered to resist the forces of sin and evil. "Not by might, nor by power, but by my spirit, saith the LORD of hosts" (Zechariah 4:6). When we are born again, we are given the gift of the Holy Spirit to help lead and guide us in truth. So, when we need strength, we can rely on the Holy Spirit to empower us to walk in the Spirit and not the flesh. Philippians 4:8-9 reminds us, "Finally, brethren, whatsoever things are true, whatsoever things are honest, whatsoever things are just, whatsoever things are pure, whatsoever things are lovely, whatsoever things are of good report; if there be any virtue, and if there be any praise, think on these things. Those things, which ye have both learned, and received, and heard, and seen in me, do, and the God of peace shall be with you."

We cannot mature spiritually if we are still holding onto things that displease our Heavenly Father. We will not be able to fulfill our purpose and destiny that God has ordained for our lives if we continue sinning. God has given us every opportunity to turn from our wicked ways and turn to Him.

Change can take place in our lives if we desire to be changed. God desires the best for our lives, but He needs willing and obedient vessels that will accept His truth and walk in His ways. God knew we would need a Savior – one who would redeem us from our sins. To show His love for us, God sent His Son, Jesus, as a living sacrifice. "For God so loved the world, that He gave His only begotten Son, that whosoever believeth in Him should not perish, but have everlasting life (John 3:16).

Jesus promised that He would not leave us alone and that He would pray to the Father to send us another Comforter. "The Counselor, the Holy Spirit, whom the Father will send in my name, will teach you all things and will remind you of everything I have said to you" (John 14:26).

Therefore, we have God the Father, Jesus the Son, and the Holy Spirit to act on our behalf. Who can go wrong with a winning team like that? It is time for us to present ourselves as living sacrifices to God. "Be imitators of God, therefore, as dearly loved children and live a life of love as Christ loved us and gave himself up for us as a fragrant offering and sacrifice to God" (Ephesians 5:1-2).

Our old habits are comfortable and can be a challenge to change. However, living a life of sin will bring destruction in our lives. "For the wages of sin is death; but the gift of God is eternal life through Jesus Christ our Lord" (Romans 6:23). When we come into the truth, we will realize that God doesn't want us to live an unfruitful, unproductive, and sinful life.

First Peter 5:8-10 tells us to:

Be self-controlled and alert. Your enemy the devil prowls around like a roaring lion looking for someone to devour. Resist him, standing firm in the faith, because you know that your brothers throughout the world are undergoing the same kind of sufferings. And the God of all grace, who called you to His eternal glory in Christ, after you have suffered a little while, will himself restore you and make you strong, firm, and steadfast.

The enemy will use any door that he can to create havoc because that is his job! He is on his job 24/7, but are we on ours? We cannot continue doing things that allow Satan to complete his mission in our lives by opening doors that are opposite of what God desires for our lives.

We are to be on guard daily. Sometimes we are quick to blame the devil for everything, but sometimes it's not him, it's us. Satan can influence, tempt, and oppress, but we have the power to choose to do what's right in the eyes of the Lord. It's our mission to keep the doors closed to sin. It's time to be honest and mature in our relationship with God and be truthful with ourselves.

We may think we have to wait to clean up our houses before we come to the Lord, but that's not so! God wants us to come to Him just as we are, and He will help us clean up the areas in our lives and make us whole, if we desire to be changed. It's a choice! God gives us freewill to choose life or death. "See, I have set before thee this day life and good, and death and evil; In that I command thee this day to love the Lord they God to walk in His ways, and to keep His commandments and His statues and His judgements that thou mayest live and multiply: and the Lord thy God shall bless thee in the land whither though goest to possess it. But if thine heart turn away, so that thou wilt not hear, but shall be drawn away, and worship other gods, and serve them; I denounce unto you this day, that ye shall surely perish, and that ye shall not prolong your days upon the land, whither thou passest over Jordan to go to possess it. I call heaven and earth to record this day against you, that I have set before you life and death, blessing and cursing: therefore choose life, that both thou and thy seed may live: That thou mayest love the Lord thy God, and that thou mayest obey His voice, and that thou may cleave unto Him: for He is thy life, and the length of thy days: that thou mayest dwell in the land which the Lord sware unto thy fathers, to Abraham, to Isaac, and to Jacob, to give them (Deuteronomy 30:15).

We need God's help to change. We can't change ourselves on our own. If we could, most of us would have already done it. God says in Ezekiel 11:19-20, "I will give them an undivided heart and put a new spirit in them; I will remove their heart of stone and give them a heart of flesh. Then they will follow my decrees and be careful to keep my laws. They will be my people and I will be their God."

The good news is that we don't have to stay where we are. Jesus took on every sin that we could ever commit when He was nailed to the cross. We simply need to open our minds and hearts to God and the truth of His Word. God can and will forgive our sins, but it's up to us to make the decision to change. Don't miss out on what God can do for you today.

Chapter 8

No More Compromising

♦ ♦ ♦ ♦ ♦ ♦ ♦

Do not merely listen to the word, and so deceive yourselves.
Do what it says.
James 1:22

It's time out for straddling the fence. We need to let our "yes" mean "yes" and our "no" mean "no." We can't be on both sides of the fence. We must decide who we will serve, Satan or God. We can either choose to walk in darkness or in light. We cannot have it both ways. James 1:7-8 tells us "that man should not think he will receive anything from the Lord; he is a double-minded man, unstable in all he does." If we are going to serve God, we must make a commitment to follow Him.

God is love, and He doesn't want His children to miss out on where He wants to take them. That is why it is so important that we hear His spiritual call to get our houses in order. If what we've been doing for the last year, five, ten, fifteen, or twenty years and etc.., hasn't worked, then it's time for change and do things God's way.

It's time to get serious about the Father's business. In Revelation 3:15-16, God went on to tell the church in Laodicea: "I know your deeds, that you are neither cold or hot. I wish you were either one or the other! So because you are lukewarm—neither hot nor cold—I am about to spit you out of my mouth."

It's time to make a conscious decision to no longer compromise our relationship with God. We must keep our eyes on Jesus and strive to walk in righteousness and holiness. Remember, this is our individual walk with the Lord. The Bible says in Philippians 2:12, "Continue to work out your salvation with fear and trembling." Don't allow sin to sway you from God's purpose and order for your life. God has a set order and standard for His children to live by, and He desires that we return to His truth and follow His way.

> Galatians 5:16-26 says:
>
> So I say, live by the Spirit, and you will not gratify the desires of the sinful nature. For the sinful nature desires what is contrary to the Spirit, and the Spirit what is contrary to the sinful nature. They are in conflict with each other, so that you do not do what you want. But if you are led by the Spirit, you are not under the law. The acts of the sinful nature are obvious: sexual immorality, impurity, and debauchery; idolatry and witchcraft; hatred, discord, jealousy, fits of rage, selfish ambition, dissensions, factions and envy; drunkenness, orgies, and the like. I warn you, as I did before, that those who live like this will not inherit the kingdom of God. But the fruit of the Spirit is love, joy,

peace, patience, kindness, goodness, faithfulness, gentleness, and self-control. Against such things there is no law. Those who belong to Christ Jesus have crucified the sinful nature with its passions and desires. Since we live by the Spirit, let us keep in step with the Spirit. Let us not become conceited, provoking, and envying each other.

We cannot allow our ears and eyes to be entertained by those things that displease God. If the music we are listening to and the movies or shows we are watching are filled with profanity, perversion, excessive violence, and sex, then change the channel. God is not pleased when we watch and listen to things that are defiled and immoral. How can we resist the devil or be self-controlled if our ears and eyes are entertained with things that are sinful? Resisting sin is much easier when you spend time with God, read His word, and obey His voice. It doesn't mean you won't be tempted; it means that you need Holy Spirit to help you overcome in an area you are struggling with.

It is our Christian and moral duty to protect not just our spirit, but the spiritual well-being of our children and other minors in our care. Since Christian parents are accountable to God for the well-being and spiritual development of their children, we need to educate and guard our children against listening and viewing things that are not pleasing to God. Parents should be mindful of the music their children are listening to, the television shows they watch, and their Internet and cell phone usage. As parents, we have a responsibility to teach children the ways of the Lord. The Bible tells parents to teach children the Word of God. "Teach them to your children, talking about them when you sit at home and when you walk along the road, when you lie down and when you get up (Deuteronomy 11:19).

God wants to do great things for the body of Christ. He is calling forth a nation, a people who will declare the works of the Lord and walk in obedience. In order for us to receive what God is proclaiming and has proclaimed for our lives, we have to get onboard with the move of God. God is looking for people who are ready to go all the way with Him. Colossians 3:5-10 tells us to:

> Put to death, therefore, whatever belongs to your earthly nature: sexual immorality, impurity, lust, evil desires, and greed, which is idolatry. Because of this, the wrath of God is coming. You used to walk in these ways, in the life you once lived. But now you must rid yourselves of all such things as these: anger, rage, malice, slander, and filthy language from your lips. Do not lie to each other since you have taken off your old self with its practices and have put on the new self, which is being renewed in knowledge in the image of its Creator.

We must repent for our sinful behaviors and crucify our flesh, because we don't know the day or the hour when the Lord will return or call our name. Therefore, we want to be ready! Some Christians may think this message is hard, but it's a love message to the body of Christ so we can be ready for His return. Luke 12:38-40 tells us, "It will be good for those servants whose master finds them ready, even if he comes in the second or third watch of the night. But understand this: If the owner of the house had known at what hour the thief was coming, he would not have let his house be broken into. You must be also ready, because the Son of Man will come at an hour when you do not expect him."

"For the Lord himself will come down from heaven, with a loud command with the voice of the archangel and with the trumpet call of God, and the dead in Christ will rise first. After that, we who are still alive and are left will be caught up together with them in the clouds to meet the Lord in the air. And so we will be with the Lord forever (1 Thessalonians 4:16-17).

Romans 6:21-23 says, "What benefit did you reap at that time from the things that you are now ashamed of? Those things resulted in death! **But now that you have been set free from sin and have become slaves to God, the benefit you reap leads to holiness, and the result is eternal life. For the wages of sin is death, but the gift of God is eternal life in Christ Jesus our Lord.**"

Knowing these things, will you be a spiritual house where God can dwell, or will you be the house that God passes by? Will you be the church (the people) that God will spew out of His mouth, or will you be the church that is spotless, blemish free, and found acceptable unto God?

Chapter 9

Repentance

♦ ♦ ♦ ♦ ♦ ♦ ♦

If my people, who are called by my name, will humble themselves and
pray and seek my face and turn from their wicked ways, then will I
hear from heaven and will forgive their sin and heal their land.
2 Chronicles 7:14

God is calling for repentance and order among the body of Christ. It's time to repent and ask God to forgive us for not being the church, the people, He has called us to be. The good news is that God is so merciful, loving, and gracious that He gives us opportunities to repent and get back on course. God gives us an example of His merciful love as He deals with Jonah and the people of Nineveh (Jonah 3:10).

God sent Jonah to Nineveh to tell the Ninevites that they would be destroyed. But God did not destroy them because they made a decision to repent and turn from their evil ways. The king made a declaration to the people of Nineveh. Jonah 3:7-9 tells us that this is the proclamation he issued in Nineveh: "By the decree of the king and his nobles: Do not let man or beast, herd or flock, taste anything; do not let them eat or drink. But let man and beast be covered with sackcloth. Let everyone call urgently on God. Let them give up their evil ways and their violence. Who knows? God may yet relent and with compassion turn from his fierce anger so that we will not perish."

I believe if we, as the body of Christ, will repent, fast, and turn from our evil ways, God will forgive our sins and bring healing to the land just as he did for Nineveh. The prophet Joel also mentions the importance of repenting for our sins. Joel 2:12-13 says, "Even now, declares the Lord, return to me with all your heart with fasting and mourning. Rend your heart and not your garments. Return to the Lord your God for he is gracious and compassionate, slow to anger and abounding in love, and he relents from sending calamity." The Bible tells us in 2 Chronicles 7:14, "If my people, who are called by my name, will humble themselves and pray and seek my face and turn from their wicked ways, then will I hear from heaven and will forgive their sin and heal their land." We have the answer; we must turn to God and do what He is requiring us to do in 2 Chronicles 7:14.

We have a nation that is starving and looking for truth. People are hurting and experiencing difficulties throughout the world. We need to show them our God, a loving and compassionate God who can restore peace in times of trouble, offer hope to the hopeless, heal the hurting and sick, and save those who are lost.

If we, the body of Christ, don't rise up and pray for repentance for the nation, who will do it? In order for God to answer our prayers, change must start with us. Our hearts must turn to Him. God hears the prayers of a righteous person. James 5:16 (KJV) confirms, "Confess your faults one to another, and pray one for another, that ye may be healed. The effectual fervent prayer of a righteous man availeth much."

For change to take place within us, we must examine the contents of our hearts. God knows our hearts, and nothing is hidden from Him. One of the definitions of the heart describes it as being the "center of one's being, feelings and emotions."

Our hearts can store feelings of love, hate, peace, joy, anger, kindness, envy, greed, gentleness, contentment, jealousy, malice, strife, forgiveness, unforgiveness, and the like. The question is, what is stored in your heart?

Whatever we have stored in our hearts will be displayed in our actions. Any negative or unresolved issues from our past will manifest in our lives. These things will show up in our conversations, emotions, behaviors, thoughts, attitudes, and how we respond and treat others. We must get to the root of our sinful hearts. If someone has hurt you or done you wrong, intentionally, or unintentionally, and you have not forgiven them, it's time to forgive and release them from your heart so you can walk in freedom. If you need help to forgive, God will help you. He's only a prayer away. "For if ye forgive men their trespasses, your heavenly Father will also forgive you. But if ye forgive not men their trespasses neither will your Father forgive your trespasses (Matthew 6:14-15).

As we refer to the heart, Luke 6:45 tells us that "the good man brings good things out of the good stored up in his heart, and the evil man brings evil things out of the evil stored up in his heart. For out of the overflow of his heart his mouth speaks." It's imperative that we take the time to examine our hearts so that we can be effective for the Kingdom of God. We can't allow ourselves to be so busy doing things in our churches that we don't take the time to evaluate what's in our hearts.

In Psalm 51:10 -13, we see David asking God's help to address the issues of his heart. He said, "Create in me a clean heart, O God, and renew a right spirit within me. Cast me not away from thy presence; and take not they Holy Spirit from me. Restore unto me the joy of thy salvation; and uphold me with thy free spirit. Then will I teach transgressors thy ways; and sinners shall be converted unto thee." Most of us know that David had sinned numerous times. He recognized the condition of his heart and knew he could not function with a soiled heart. He knew his desires, thoughts, and behaviors did not line up with God's heart. He cried for God to do spiritual surgery on his heart.

Just like David, we can no longer be driven by our sinful nature. We must ask God for a new heart. A changed heart. "I will give you a new heart and put a new spirit in you; I will remove from you your heart of stone and give you a heart of flesh" (Ezekiel 36:26). We need to pray for a heart that is filled with the love and compassion that pleases God. A heart that is open to loving our neighbor, loving ourselves, quick to forgive, obedient to the voice of the Lord, and a heart for the unsaved.

"The heart is deceitful above all things, and desperately wicked: who can know it?" (Jeremiah 17:9, KJV). "Oh, that their hearts would be inclined to fear me and keep all my commands always, so that it might go well with them and their children forever" (Deuteronomy 5:29).

Chapter 10

Deliverance Must Take Place

♦ ♦ ♦ ♦ ♦ ♦ ♦

"How can one enter into a strong man's house, and spoil his goods,
except he first bind the strong man? and then he will spoil his house."
(Matthew 12:20)

I believe one of the hardest things for a believer to do is to admit he or she needs to be delivered. It is so much easier to look at someone else's issues, but when you have to take a look at yourself and your behaviors, the pill is harder to swallow. However, we must be truthful with ourselves. In order for us to live the life God has called us to live and be effective for the Kingdom of God, we must take the time to allow the Holy Spirit to expose what's hidden in our hearts. Many times, we are holding onto unresolved issues that are deeply rooted and are leading our behaviors.

Deliverance is the action of being rescued from something, the consequences of sin and being set free. Deliverance may not always be automatic. It can be a process. Everyone's experience is different. Most of the time some of the problems we are dealing with originated from our childhood or painful situations we have experienced as a teenager or adult. The effects of negative words, disappointments, inappropriate touches, abuse, neglect, rejection, hurt, abandonment, shame, losses, emotional hurt, and pain has the potential to impact our lives.

The first step to resolving an issue is to be honest with yourself and admit there is a problem. If you are unsure of an area of your life that needs deliverance, ask the Holy Spirit to reveal it. The second step is doing something about it, and the third step is to realize you need God's help, because He is the Deliverer.

For deliverance to begin, you must be honest with yourself and evaluate the areas in your life that continues to be unfruitful, sinful and are hindering you from overcoming in that area. God can deliver you! Sometimes deliverance can take place with just you and God. However, if you need additional assistance with deliverance, pray for God to lead you to a deliverance ministry or a deliverance minister. I remember watching a bishop on the internet during his morning church service. The Spirit of God was high, and the Word was rich. The more the man of God preached, the more I began to weep and cry out to God. God began revealing the hurt and pain that I occurred from my childhood that affected my adult life and the choices that I made. Healing and deliverance took place for me on that day! I was set free, because God revealed truth to me. That was just one of the ways I've experienced deliverance, there were others. God is not limited. God can lead you into deliverance by anyway He chooses. All

God needs is your participation, and the Spirit of God will do the rest. Don't be ashamed to admit that you need deliverance.

Once the Spirit of God delivers you in an area, keep the door closed to that thing you were delivered from and allow yourself to be filled with the peace and love of God.

You have the power to say no to the past and not go back into the door from which you were delivered from. Stay free! Keep your heart pure and your house (temple) clean. Your body is the temple for the Holy Spirit. *"Do you not know that your bodies are temples of the Holy Spirit, who is in you, who you have received from God? You are not your own; you were brought at a price. Therefore, honor God with your bodies"* (1 Corinthians 6:19-20). And if you happen to fall, get back up again, repent quickly, and keep striving toward the mark of Christ Jesus and ask God to give you strength to walk it out. Don't allow condemnation to hold you back. Keep looking forward because God judges the heart and not your outward appearance. Holy Spirit will bring about conviction, but not condemnation.

When Jesus returns, He will be looking for a glorious church. Jesus is not coming back for a building. He is coming back for His people. He is coming back for us! First Thessalonians 4:16-17 states, "For the Lord himself will come down from heaven, with a loud command, with the voice of the archangel and with the trumpet call of God, and the dead in Christ will rise first. After that, we who are still alive and are left will be caught up together with them in the clouds to meet the Lord in the air. And so we will be with the Lord forever."

In the next chapter you will find steps in taking inventory of your house and a deliverance prayer that will help you with that process. I've also included a salvation and rededication prayer for those who desire to accept salvation and/or rededicate their life back to Jesus Christ.

Taking Inventory of Your House

♦ ♦ ♦ ♦ ♦ ♦ ♦ ♦ ♦ ♦

Listed below you will find an inventory checklist of the sinful nature. Check off those areas that you are aware of and pray and ask God to reveal what other areas maybe hidden in your heart.

After taking the inventory checklist you will find a prayer for salvation and rededication, and a prayer for repentance & deliverance to use as a guide, if needed. If not, allow the Holy Spirit to guide your prayer.

You will also find supporting scriptural references and a glossary located at the back of the book.

Untamed Tongues

_____ Backbiting: To speak spitefully or slanderously about another.
_____ Cursing: Profane word or phrase.
_____ Gossiping: Rumor or talk of a person, which is of a sensational and intimate nature.
_____ Lying: A false statement deliberately presented as being true.
_____ Quarreling: An angry dispute or an altercation.

_____ Slandering: Oral communication of false statements injurious to person's reputation.

Uncontrolled Emotions

_____ Anger: A strong feeling of displeasure of hostility.

_____ Anxious: Extreme uneasiness of mind or fear of something.

_____ Arrogant: Conceited, having an exaggerated sense of one's own importance or abilities, self-important.

_____ Bitterness: Harshness, marked by resentment, cynicism, or anger.

_____ Discord: Tension or strife resulting from a lack of agreement.

_____ Dissension: A difference of opinions; one leading to an uprising.

_____ Envy: A feeling of discontent and resentment aroused by the desire for the possession or qualities of another.

_____ Haughty: Pompous, vain, prideful, snobbish, arrogant, uppity.

_____ Malice: Being spiteful because of jealousy.

_____ Greed: An excessive desire to acquire or possess more than one needs or deserves.

_____ Hatred: Intense animosity or hostility.

_____ Haste: When an action is made too quickly to be accurate or wise.

_____ Impulsive: Inclined to act on impulse rather than thought.

_____ Jealousy: Resentment or bitterness in rivalry; envious.

_____ Pride: A pleasure from one's own achievement. A proud person is haughty, arrogant, conceited, vain, or boastful.

_____ Rage: A sudden outburst of emotion; violently explosive anger; furious intensity; uncontrolled anger.

_____ Resentment: Indignation or ill will felt as a result of a real or imagined grievance.

____ Selfish ambition: An eager or strong desire to achieve something for oneself; excessive desire for honor, power, or

wealth.

____ Unforgiving: Reluctance or refusal to forgive.

Sexual Immoralities

____ Adultery: Voluntary sexual intercourse between a married person and partner other than the lawful spouse.

____ Fornication: Sexual intercourse between two partners who are not married to each other.

____ Homosexuality: Having sexual orientation to persons of the same sex. A homosexual person is a gay man or lesbian

woman.

____ Lust: An intense or unrestrained sexual craving.

____ Masturbation: Manually stimulation of one's own genitals, or with the use of an instrument, for sexual pleasure.

____ Pornography: Sexually explicit materials used for sexual excitement.

Sinful Behaviors

You can write down any other sinful behaviors that God has
revealed to you.

_____

_____

_____

_____

_____

_____

_____

_____

_____

_____

_____

Prayer of Salvation/Rededication

♦ ♦ ♦ ♦ ♦ ♦ ♦

Father God, I confess that I am a sinner and I repent of my sins. Romans 10:9, says, that if I shall confess with my mouth the Lord Jesus, and shall believe in my heart that God hath raised him from the dead I shall be saved. I believe in my heart that Jesus Christ is Lord and that He shed His blood on the cross for my sins. I accept His love and forgiveness for my sins. Lord Jesus, I ask You to come into my heart, save me, and cleanse me from all unrighteousness. I invite Holy Spirit into my life to guide and lead me into all truth. I dedicate my life to You. I thank You that I am saved and set free in Jesus Christ's name. Amen.

Prayer of Repentance & Deliverance

♦ ♦ ♦ ♦ ♦ ♦ ♦ ♦ ♦ ♦ ♦ ♦ ♦ ♦

Father God, I give you permission to search my heart and remove

anything that's doesn't please You. I ask that You forgive my sins

and help me to forgive others. Give me a pure heart and renew a

right spirit within me. I thank You for Your Son, Jesus, and what

He did for me on the cross. I thank You for salvation, and the

blood that Jesus shed on my behalf. I invite Holy Spirit into my life

to rule, reign and order my steps every day of my life. I thank You

that I no longer gratify my sinful nature, but I walk in the fruit of

the Spirit which are love, joy, peace, patience, kindness, goodness,

faithfulness, gentleness, and self-control. I renounce and denounce

my sinful way of living! I am no longer bound by: (list the

behaviors/sins you are struggling with and call them out one by one), _____, _____,

_____, because I am set free in Jesus Name!

I shut the door to demonic oppression, interferences, and

influences in the Name of Jesus! I plead the blood of Jesus Christ

over my life and no weapon formed against me shall prosper in

Jesus Name! I thank you Father that through the blood of Jesus

Christ, I am healed, delivered, and set free. I thank you Lord,

because I am no longer captive to the captivity of sin. For whom

the Son sets free, is free indeed!   I thank You for a brand-new day

and a new beginning in You! A new way to live! A new direction!

In Jesus Name, Amen!

Scriptural References

♦ ♦ ♦ ♦ ♦ ♦ ♦ ♦ ♦

UNTAMED TONGUE

BACKBITING

Proverbs 25:23 (KJV)
The north wind driveth away rain: so doth an angry countenance a backbiting tongue.

CURSING

Romans 3:13-14
Their throats are open graves; their tongues practice deceit. The poison of vipers is on their lips. Their mouths are full of cursing and bitterness.

James 3:10
Out of the same mouth come praising and cursing. My brothers, that should not be.

GOSSIPPING

Proverbs 20:19
A gossip betrays a confidence, so avoid a man who talks too much.

Proverbs 16:28
A perverse person stirs up conflict, and a gossip separates close friends.

Proverbs 26:20
Without wood a fire goes out: without gossip a quarrel dies down.

LYING

Proverbs 12:22
The Lord detests lying lips, but he delights in people who are trustworthy.

Proverbs 26:28
A lying tongue hates those it hurts, and a flattering mouth works ruin.

PRIDE

Proverbs 16:18
Pride goes before destruction, a haughty spirit before a fall.

Proverbs 8:13
To fear the LORD is to hate evil; I hate pride and arrogance, evil behavior and perverse speech.

QUARRELING

1 Corinthians 3:3
You are still worldly. For since there is jealousy and quarreling among you, are you not worldly? Are you not acting like mere men?

2 Corinthians 12:20
For I am afraid that when I come, I may not find you as I want you to be, and you may not find me as you want me to be. I fear that there may be quarreling, jealousy, outbursts of anger, factions, slander, gossip, arrogance and disorder.

Proverbs 15:18
A hot-tempered man stirs up dissension, but a patient man calms a quarrel.

SLANDER

Leviticus 19:16
Do not go about spreading slander among your people. Do not do anything that endangers your neighbor's life. I am the LORD.

Proverbs 10:18
He who conceals his hatred has lying lips, and whoever spreads slander is a fool.

UNCONTROLLED EMOTIONS

ANGER

Proverbs 29:11
A fool gives full vent to his anger, but a wise man keeps himself under control.

Ephesians 4:26
In your anger do not sin: Do not let the sun go down while you are still angry.

ARROGANCE

Romans 12:3
For by the grace given me I say to every one of you: Do not think of yourself more highly than you ought, but rather think of yourself with sober judgment, in accordance with the faith God has distributed to each of you.

Proverbs 16:5
The Lord detests all the proud of the heart. Be sure of this: They will not go unpunished.

BITTERNESS

Hebrews 12:15
See to it that no one misses the grace of God and that no bitter root grows up to cause trouble and defile many.

Ephesians 4:31
Get rid of all bitterness, rage and anger, brawling and slander, along with every form of malice.

DISSENSION

Proverbs 6:14
Who plots evil with deceit in his heart—he always stirs up dissension.

Proverbs 15:18
A hot-tempered man stirs up dissension, but a patient man calms a quarrel.

Proverbs 6:16-19 (KJV)
These six things doth the LORD hate: yea, seven are an abomination unto him: A proud look, a lying tongue, and hands that shed innocent blood, An heart that deviseth wicked imaginations, feet that be swift in running to mischief, A false witness that speaketh lies, and he that soweth discord among brethren.

DISCORD

Galatians 5:19–21
The acts of the sinful nature are obvious: sexual immorality, impurity and debauchery, idolatry and witchcraft; hatred, discord, jealousy, fits of rage, selfish ambition, dissensions, factions, and envy; drunkenness, orgies, and the like. I warn you, as I did before, that those who live like this will not inherit the kingdom of God.

ENVY

Proverbs 14:30
A heart at peace gives life to the body, but envy rots the bones.

James 3:14-16
But if you harbor bitter envy and selfish ambition in your hearts, do not boast about it or deny the truth. Such wisdom does not come from heaven but is earthly, unspiritual, of the devil. For where you have envy and selfish ambition, there you find disorder and every evil practice.

GREED

Colossians 3:5
Put to death, therefore, whatever belongs to your earthly nature: sexual immorality, impurity, lust, evil desires and greed, which is idolatry.

Proverbs 15:27
A greedy man brings trouble to his family, but he who hates bribes will live.

HASTE/IMPULSIVE

Philippians 4:6
Do not be anxious about anything, but in everything, by prayer and petition, with thanksgiving, present your requests to God.

HATRED

Leviticus 19:17
Do not hate your brother in your heart. Rebuke your neighbor frankly so that you will not share in his guilt.

Proverbs 10:12
Hatred stirs up dissension, but love covers over all wrongs.

HAUGHTY

Proverbs 16:28
Pride goes before destruction, a haughty spirit before a fall.

Isaiah 13:11
I will punish the world for its evil, the wicked for their sins. I will put an end to the arrogance of the haughty and will humble the pride of the ruthless.

IDOLATRY

1 Corinthians 10:14
Therefore, my dear friends, flee from idolatry.

Colossians 3:5
Put to death, therefore, whatever belongs to your earthly nature: sexual immorality, impurity, lust, evil desires, and greed, which is idolatry.

JEALOUSY

1 Corinthians 3:3
You are still worldly. For since there is jealousy and quarrelling among you, are you not worldly? Are you not acting like mere man?

2 Corinthians 12:20
For I am afraid that when I come I may not find you as I want you to be, and you may not find me as you want me to be. I fear that there may be quarreling, jealousy, outbursts of anger, factions, slander, gossip, arrogance and disorder.

RAGE

Colossians 3:8
But now you must rid yourselves of all such things as these: anger, rage, malice, slander, and filthy language from your lips.

Ephesians 4:31
Get rid of all bitterness, rage and anger, brawling and slander along with every form of malice.

RESENTMENT

Job 5:2
Resentment kills a fool, and envy slays the simple.

Job 36:13 (KJV)
But the hypocrites in heart heap up wrath: they cry not when he bindeth them.

SELFISH AMBITIONS

Philippians 2:3
Do nothing out of selfish ambitions or vain conceit, but in humility consider others better than yourselves.

James 3:16
For where you have envy and selfish ambition, there you find disorder and every evil practice.

UNFORGIVENESS

Matthew 6:14-15
For if you forgive men when they sin against you, your heavenly Father will also forgive you. But if you do not forgive men their sins, your Father will not forgive your sins.

Matthew 18:34-35

In anger his master turned him over to the jailers to be tortured, until he should pay back all he owed. This is how my heavenly Father will treat each of you unless you forgive your brother from your heart.

SEXUAL IMMORALITIES

ADULTERY

Exodus 20:14
You shall not commit adultery.

Matthew 5:28
I tell you that anyone who looks at a woman lustfully has already committed adultery with lust in her his heart.

FORNICATION

1 Corinthians 6:13
Food for the stomach and the stomach for food—but God will destroy them both. The body is not meant for sexual immorality, but for the Lord, and the Lord for the body.

1 Corinthians 6:18-20
Flee from sexual immorality. All other sins a man commits are outside his body, but he who sins sexually sins against his own body. Do you not know that your body is a temple of the Holy Spirit, who is in you whom you have received from God? You are not your own; you were brought at a price. Therefore, honor God with your body.

HOMOSEXUALITY

1 Corinthians 6:9-10
Do you not know that the wicked will not inherit the kingdom of God? Do not be deceived: Neither the sexually immoral nor

idolaters nor adulterers nor men who have sex with men nor thieves nor the greedy nor drunkards nor slanderers nor swindlers will inherit the kingdom of God.

Romans 1:26-27
Because of this, God gave them over to shameful lusts. Even their women exchanged natural relations for unnatural ones. In the same way the men also abandoned natural relations with women and were inflamed with lust for one another. Men committed indecent acts with other men and received in themselves due penalty for their perversion.

LUST

Ephesians 4:19
Having lost all sensitivity, they have given themselves over to sensuality so as to indulge in every kind of impurity, with a continual lust for more.

1 Peter 4:3
For you have spent enough time in the past doing what pagans choose to do—living in debauchery, lust, drunkenness, orgies, carousing, and detestable idolatry.

Ephesians 5:3
But among you there must not be even a hint of sexual immorality, or of any kind of impurity, or of greed, because these are improper for God's holy people.

1 Thessalonians 4:3-5
It is God's will that you be sanctified that you should avoid sexual immorality; that each of you should learn to control his own body in a way that is holy and honorable not in passionate lust like the heathen who do not know God.

FRUIT OF THE SPIRIT

LOVE

1 Peter 4: 8
Above all, love each other deeply, because love covers over a multitude of sins.

John 13:34-35
A new command I give you: Love one another. As I have loved you, so you must love one another. By this all men will know that you are my disciples, if you love one another.

1 John 3:18
Dear children, let us not love with words or tongue but with actions and in truth.

1 John 4:11
Dear friends, since God so loved us, we also ought to love one another.

JOY

Psalm 68:3
But may the righteous be glad and rejoice before God; may they be happy and joyful.

John 15:11
I have told you this so that my joy may be in you and that your joy may be complete.

Nehemiah 8:10
Nehemiah said, "Go and enjoy choice food and sweet drinks, and send some to those who have nothing prepared. This day is sacred to our Lord. Do not grieve, for the joy of the LORD is your strength."

PEACE

Colossians 3:15
Let the peace of Christ rule in your hearts, since as members of one body you were called to peace. And be thankful.

Philippians 4:7
And the peace of God, which transcends all understanding, will guard your hearts and your minds in Christ Jesus.

John 14:27
Peace I leave with you; my peace I give you. I do not give to you as the world gives. Do not let your hearts be troubled and do not be afraid.

PATIENCE

Galatians 6:9
Let us not become weary in doing good, for at the proper time we will reap a harvest if we do not give up.

James 1:2-4 (KJV)
My brethren, count it all joy when ye fall into divers temptations; Knowing this, that the trying of your faith worketh patience. But let patience have her perfect work, that ye may be perfect and entire, wanting nothing.

KINDNESS

Colossians 3:12-13
Therefore, as God's chosen people, holy and dearly loved, clothe yourselves with compassion, kindness, humility, gentleness and patience. Bear with each other and forgive whatever grievances you may have against one another. Forgive as the Lord forgave you.

Romans 12:9-10

Love must be sincere. Hate what is evil; cling to what is good. Be devoted to one another in brotherly love. Honor one another above yourselves.

GOODNESS

Ephesians 5:9
For the fruit of the light consists in all goodness, righteousness and truth.

2 Peter 1:3
His divine power has given us everything we need for life and godliness through our knowledge of him who called us by his own glory and goodness.

2 Peter 1:5-7
For this very reason, make every effort to add to your faith goodness; and to goodness, knowledge; and to knowledge, self-control; and to self-control, perseverance; and to perseverance, godliness; and to godliness, brotherly kindness; and to brotherly kindness, love.

FAITHFULNESS

Mark 11:22-23 (KJV)
And Jesus answering saith unto them, Have faith in God. For verily I say unto you, That whosoever shall say unto this mountain, Be thou removed, and be thou cast into the sea; and shall not doubt in his heart, but shall believe that those things which he saith shall come to pass; he shall have whatsoever he saith.

2 Corinthians 5:7
We live by faith, not by sight.

James 1:5-6
If any of you lacks wisdom, he should ask God, who gives generously to all without finding fault, and it will be given to him.

But when he asks, he must believe and not doubt, because he who doubts is like a wave of the sea, blown and tossed by the wind.

GENTLENESS

Philippians 4:5
Let your gentleness be evident to all. The Lord is near.

Colossians 3:12
Therefore, as God's chosen people, holy and dearly loved, clothe yourselves with compassion, kindness, humility, gentleness and patience.

1 Peter 3:14-16
But even if you should suffer for what is right, you are blessed. Do not fear what they fear; do not be frightened. But in your hearts set apart Christ as Lord. Always be prepared to give an answer to everyone who asks you to give the reason for the hope that you have. But do this with gentleness and respect, keeping a clear conscience, so that those who speak maliciously against your good behavior in Christ may be ashamed of their slander.

SELF-CONTROL

1 Thessalonians 5:6
So then, let us not be like others, who are asleep, but let us be alert and self-controlled.

1 Thessalonians 5:8
But since we belong to the day, let us be self-controlled, putting on faith and love as a breastplate, and the hope of salvation as a helmet.

Glossary
♦ ♦ ♦

Abomination: A thing thoroughly detested; disgusting, unclean, to be a moral stench.

Celibacy: The practice of sexual abstinence.

Church: A congregation. The company of all Christians regarded as a spiritual body or a building for public, especially Christian worship.

Confession: To acknowledge sin, faith, or belief.

Deliverance: The act of being set free.

Emotion: An intense mental state that arises subjectively rather than through conscious effort; a strong feeling.

Flesh: Human nature (carnal man).

Grace: Unmerited favor or virtue from God.

Holiness: The state of being holy (religious and morally good).

House: A dwelling place; temple.

Forgiveness: The renouncing of anger or resentment against someone. To excuse for a fault or an offense.

Holy Spirit: The third person of the Christianity Trinity. The Spirit of God.

Idolatry: The worship of a physical object as a god.

Immoral: Contrary to established moral principles.

Impurity: The quality or condition of being impure, contamination. State of immorality; sin.

Inherit: To be an heir. To gain something as one's right or portion.

Kingdom: The eternal spiritual sovereignty of God. A realm of rulership and dominion.

Mind: The human consciousness that originates in the brain and is manifested especially in thought, perception, emotion, will, memory, and imagination.

Patience: The quality of being able to calmly await an outcome or a result, not hasty or impulsive.

Repentance: A turning back. To make a change for the better as a result of remorse or contrition of one's sins.

Righteous: Following religious or moral laws. Acting in accordance with divine or moral law, free from guilt of sin.

Salvation: To make free, liberty. Deliverance from the power or penalty of sin, redemption.

Saved: To be set free from the consequences of sin; to be redeemed.

Sin: Deliberate disobedience to the known will of God.

Temple: A sacred dwelling place.

Uncleanness: To be morally contaminated, impure, common, blemished, or disgraced.

Will: The mental faculty by which one deliberately chooses a course of action.

Wrath: Forceful and often vindictive anger. Punishment or vengeance as a manifestation of anger.

About the Author, Pamela Wakefield

♦ ♦ ♦ ♦ ♦ ♦

Pamela Wakefield is an ordained evangelist, woman of faith, intercessor, author and entrepreneur. Pamela is passionate about writing and writes from her heart. Her desire is that her writing will bring about change in the lives of her readers. Pamela is a mother and grandmother who resides in Raleigh, North Carolina. For more information about Pamela, and/or to purchase her books you can email her at pamelawakefield03@gmail.com.

Notes:

Notes:

Notes:

Notes:

www.ingramcontent.com/pod-product-compliance
Lightning Source LLC
Chambersburg PA
CBHW021242090426
42740CB00006B/656